Hanging by a Thread

The Questions of the Cross

Samuel Wells

Church Publishing
NEW YORK

First published in the United Kingdom in 2016 by the
Canterbury Press Norwich
Editorial office
3rd Floor, Invicta House
108–114 Golden Lane
London EC1Y 0TG, UK

Canterbury Press is an imprint of Hymns Ancient & Modern Ltd
(a registered charity)

13A Hellesdon Park Road, Norwich
Norfolk NR6 5DR, UK
www.canterburypress.co.uk

First published in the United States in 2017 by
Church Publishing
19 East 34th Street
New York, NY 10016
www.churchpublishing.org

Cover design by Jennifer Kopec, 2Pug Design

Library of Congress Cataloging-in-Publication Data

A record of this book is available from the Library of Congress

ISBN-13: 978-0-89869-977-7 (pbk.)
ISBN-13: 978-0-89869-100-9 (ebook)

Printed in the United States of America

Hanging by a Thread

For Karl

Contents

Introduction

There was a time when the cross was an answer. For the early Church the cross explained why there needed to be a Church at all: Israel had rejected Jesus the Messiah, and the Roman Empire had killed him – so a new institution, neither chosen people nor worldwide superpower, arose to worship the crucified Lord. For Christendom (the many centuries in which Church and state asked the same questions and reached the same conclusions) the cross explained how God in Christ had dealt with eternal matters, leaving us to deal with earthly ones. For the time of the West's expanding empires, the cross explained why the benighted ones would one day thank us for our invasions so much: for we knew the grace of God, utterly portrayed in the crucified Jesus, and they did not.

Today the cross is no longer an answer. Today the cross is a question. It's a question about God, about existence and about us. In the days when the cross was an answer we didn't need to pay attention because we already knew the answer. The answer was that Christianity confirmed everything we already believed about existence. Now that the cross is a question we fear to pay attention because we find the question so frightening and we're terrified to face it because we are afraid it may not have an answer. And our faith will be hanging by a thread.

Some years ago, when I served at Duke University Chapel in North Carolina, I used to share in the service of Tenebrae. I found it one of the most memorable services of the year. At around 7.30 p.m. on the evening of Good Friday there would be a single reading, followed by a sermon; then, interspersed with Passiontide hymns, there would follow a series of readings, and, after each reading, one of seven huge candles placed on the altar would be snuffed out. Finally the congregation of around 1,300 would listen, in darkness and silence, as the tower bell tolled 39 times. That silence was louder than any music or words.

The question that exercised those preparing for the service was, what should happen after the great silence? The tradition had been that a candle would be brought forward slowly from the back of the chapel, more than 50 rows back, a journey taking a minute or so, and that the person bearing the candle would light a small candle that was placed to one side of the altar, at a lower level. It was a beautiful and compelling moment. The symbolism was unmistakeable: 'The light shines in the darkness, and the darkness did not overcome it' (John 1.5). From this flame, the whole world would shine in glory. God's love had been snuffed out, but you can't snuff out the nature and destiny of all things. Humbly, quietly, but relentlessly, it would reassert itself.

The trouble was, it was an action befitting a Saturday night Easter Vigil rather than a Friday night Tenebrae. It seemed to me to represent a profound reluctance to stay with the unresolved, tragic and terrifying experience of Good Friday evening. In subsequent years various endings were tried; but in the end it was decided that there could be no conclusion: the bell should toll, there should be silence; and, after a solemn interlude, there should be sufficient side-aisle lights lit to enable those who wished to do so to leave in safety.

This liturgical question goes right to the heart of the theology of Good Friday. Was the cross an agonizing, horrifying but ultimately successful and triumphant enterprise, in which a limitlessly-loving and inexpressibly-gracious saviour secured our eternal salvation by assuaging the rasping hunger of death and satisfying the just demands of recompense for sin? Or was it, rather, the tragic, cruel and ugly epitome of the world's failure to embrace the utter goodness of God embodied in Christ, an ending so shameful, so isolated, so apparently final, that it exposes the Church's deepest, yet invariably suppressed, fears about the absence, defeat or non-existence of God? If it was the former, the solemn entry of a candle is an appropriate and tender sign of completion, celebration and first-fruits of redemption. If it was the latter, the candle is a sign of our denial of the cost, risk and full horror of the cross, a hasty and perhaps shallow attempt to turn tragedy into comedy, to resist pathos and rush to a happy ending.

If Christian understanding of the cross errs on one side

or the other, it must surely be the latter. The cross does not invite us to dodge the searing questions of suffering, doubt and evil, in the assured confidence that it was all part of The Plan; instead the cross calls us to go to the bottom of the slough of despond, knowing that the resurrection (though predicted) would lose its power if anyone had seriously seen it coming. Jesus' words from the cross are the utterances of an agonized and dying man; they lose their poignancy if they're simply transposed into a story where everything comes right in the end. The cross is not an answer that leaves us comfortable and assured: it's a question that leaves our faith hanging by a thread.

Christians regard the cross as the most awful event in human history. Let's survey the scene. Here is a naked man. He's been beaten to pulp. He's bleeding hand and foot. His arms are spread-eagled so he can't fight off the flies or wipe away the sweat and the blood. He's practically alone. He's more or less isolated. He's totally humiliated. It's almost impossible to look at a picture of such agony and misery.

And at the climax of this ghastly scene, John's Gospel tells us, this man says one single word: 'Finished.' This is the word that seems to validate the upbeat version of Good Friday – the one that emphasizes the word 'Good'. Let's ponder for a moment the host of meanings of that word. Finished. The dissertation's finally edited and handed in. Finished. The marathon's run and I'm totally done in. Finished. The relationship's over and she's told me she doesn't love me. Finished. The work of art is completed and ready for display. Finished. The counselling has run its course and I can face the world without fear or bitterness or anger. Finished. I've served my sentence and I can come out of prison. Finished. I've been told I've no longer got a job and needn't come back to work. Finished.

But it's dangerous to rush too quickly to calling Good Friday 'Good'. Surely Jesus' climactic words from the cross must be ironic. This isn't the way the story was supposed to end. Consider the heavenly host of angels in the skies above Bethlehem singing of peace on earth. Surely this wasn't the way they imagined it would all turn out. Recall the crowds on Palm Sunday waving branches and shouting Hosanna. Surely they weren't thinking of this apocalypse five days later. A lot of other words might capture it. Ruined, betrayed, wasted, lost, destroyed, devastated, ravaged, spoiled, wrecked ... but not 'finished'. What might this word 'finished' mean? Let's look a little closer. Let's see if we can discover what is finished by Friday afternoon. The cross polishes off not just a facile rendition of The Plan, but almost everything else that characterizes a too-easy codification of Christianity. Let's snuff out the seven candles on that altar of superficial tidiness one by one.

One thing that's finished is the blond Jesus with the constant smile, the loose-fitting toga and the baby lamb constantly around his neck like a primal life-jacket. That would be the Jesus whose picture perched above my bed as a child. The one that loves the little children. There's nothing sentimental about the cross. There's no guitar-playing, commune-dwelling, tie-dying, knitted-yogurt-eating, country-road-singing, long-haired-lover-from-Liverpool, John-Denver-bespectacled Jesus in the face of Good Friday. Jesus is mutilated. He's taunted. He's asphyxiated. The Jesus of our projections, the kind friend, the handsome suitor, the Mr Fix-it, the husky organic farmer, the country sage, the wandering minstrel – they all die at the foot of the cross. The rose-tinted Jesus of soft-focused promotional paraphernalia is gone. Finished.

Another thing that's finished is the conquering Jesus with the righteous fist, the Jesus whom the Crusader thought he was upholding as he smashed the head of the infidel, the Jesus whom the Inquisition believed it was promoting by torture and cruelty, the Jesus proclaimed by conquistadors with colonial mind-sets and rapacious ambitions, the Jesus that demands to seize control of the government, the Jesus that obliterates other religions from the face of the earth, the Jesus whose name is invoked to justify one race or people or gender giving themselves sanction to oppress and marginalize and laud it over others. On Good Friday Jesus doesn't conquer. He's humiliated. He's defeated. He's dragged through the streets like a slave or a dog. The Jesus that gives credibility to human power-grabs is gone. Finished.

And that's by no means all. The Jesus that makes for good citizenship and stable social relations is finished too. Jesus died a criminal's death. We can plead his innocence as long as we like, but in the eyes of the Sanhedrin he was acting as if he was the Messiah, the Son of God, the one who was bringing Israel's long exile to an end. And that meant he had to die. And in the eyes of the Romans he was a rabble-rouser and a potential king, and that made him guilty of a capital crime. Jesus was a good citizen of the kingdom of heaven, but not a very reliable citizen of Rome. So the meek Jesus that believes in law and order, the mild Jesus that instructs children to be good and kind and to obey their parents, the Jesus that doesn't want to rock the political boat or disturb the neighbours – that Jesus dies in the face of the cross. That Jesus is finished.

And what about the Jesus of The Plan, the Jesus of the mathematical equation – the Jesus that says, 'Take one drop of total human depravity, add one pinch of utter divine grace, mix with one broken law and blend in one innocent death, and then subtract one angry devil'? That Jesus, who seems subject to some extraneous logic invisible to the eyes of the disciples but obvious to the well-informed cosmic legal historian, that Jesus disintegrates in the face of the circumstantial detail of the cross. If Jesus were simply a component in a mathematical equation or legal formula that got us off the devil's hook, then why would the Gospels tell us so much about the disciples who deserted him, the women who followed him, the mother who loved him, the sinners he forgave, the sick he healed, the poor he accompanied, the blind he led? By the time we get to the cross the Gospels have shown us enough about Jesus not just to show us how much he loves us but to make us love him. You don't love a formula or an equation. The cross shows us not forensic symmetry but wondrous love. The Jesus of the divine bargain is finished.

And then there's the Jesus that watches idly by while

earthquakes destroy countries, while ISIS and Al-Qaeda plague a generation, while civil war becomes a way of life across the world, while loved ones develop cancer, while drought afflicts continents, while hurricanes and tsunamis wreck households and livelihoods and cities. Nero watched from afar and fiddled while Rome burned; but Jesus isn't looking idly through some heavenly telescope. Jesus is suffering an agony as bad as any known to human experience. Jesus isn't tucked up in the sky, peering down from a safe distance: he's in the middle of a human train-crash, the glass and wheels and rails and twisted metal all contorting his body and piercing his soul. If you ever look up to the sky and shout 'Oh God, why?' you're looking in the wrong place. You need to be looking into the face of the crucified Jesus. That distant remote-control God has got nothing to do with Christianity. In the face of Good Friday, that Jesus is finished.

And here's a painful one. The Jesus that belongs to the Church, the Jesus that gives an affirming thumbs-up to everything Christians set out to do, the Jesus that makes a congregation a circle of holiness and a cradle of wholesomeness – that Jesus withers in the face of the cross. It's not clear when the Church begins. Maybe when Jesus gives Peter the keys of the kingdom. Maybe when Jesus says to Peter, 'Feed my Sheep'. Maybe when Jesus breathes on the disciples and says, 'I send you'. Maybe when the Holy Spirit comes down at Pentecost. But a good candidate for the beginning of the Church is right here at the cross, when Jesus hands his mother over to the care of the beloved disciple. You can see Mary representing Israel and the beloved disciple representing the Church, and Jesus' instructions portraying the inextricable destiny of the two. Not a glamorous scene, is it? This is two fragile figures amid a vista of apocalyptic devastation. Not exactly a mega-church bent on growth. Lends a whole new irony to Jesus' words, 'Where two or three are gathered, I am with them', doesn't it? In the face of the cross, there's no place for the self-congratulatory Church that's holier than God. There's only a place for church that looks like Jesus. Any other Church is like any other Jesus. It's finished.

But here's the most important one of all. The cross confronts us with the fragility of Jesus. He's no superman who leaps down and says, 'Only joking!' He suffers to the end. We wonder how this awful spectacle can possibly be necessary for our salvation. We're supposed to wonder that. We wonder whether this tiny, broken, wasted body can possibly be the body of God. We're supposed to wonder that. We wonder how any joy, any hope, any glory can possibly emerge from this hideous catastrophe. We're supposed to wonder that. We wonder why God doesn't utterly reject us after we've shown the very worst that we can do. We're supposed to wonder that. All of those wonderings should be part of our faith, our imagination, our daily prayer and our compassionate hearts. But for all our wondering and pondering, one thing is utterly clear. When we see the pain, when we feel the grief, when we look upon the loneliness, when we touch the wounds, when we hear the cries, we know, we know that God will go to any lengths for us, God will never be separated from us, that loving us is written into God's DNA, that there's no part of God that has any desire to be except to be with us, that Jesus is the embodiment of the way God's destiny is wrapped up in us for ever. Any other notion of God, any other speculation about God's wishes, any other idea about what lies at the heart of God is gone. Over. Dispelled. Finished.

Jesus' final words: 'Finished.' His life is finished. His ministry's finished. The scriptures are finished. The reconciliation of God and creation is finished. And a host of misconceptions are dispatched at the same time. Jesus isn't a cosy companion. He's not a triumphalist conqueror. He's not a law-abiding do-gooder. He's not legal formula. He's not a heartless onlooker. He's not a pretext for Christian self-satisfaction. All those idolatries are finished. They're snuffed out like a line of candles, one by one. Finished. Finished. Finished. Finished. Finished. Finished. Finished.

Everything's finished. Everything's desolate. Everything's laid waste. Everything's lost, except the heart of God laid bare. And if we're not seduced by a comforting saviour, if we're not mesmerized by a merciless hero, if we're not domesticated by a model citizen, if we're not obsessed by a mathematical equation, if we're not alienated by a distant deity, if we haven't fled from the cross like most of the Church for most of its history, we might just get close enough to glimpse that sacred heart laid bare.

Conventional faith, as represented by these seven snuffed-out candles, is left hanging by a thread. I don't set out to interrogate customary models of atonement, but they do come in for quite a bit of scrutiny in these pages, because my understanding of the cross resists any account of salvation that's tidier and cleaner and more assured than Jesus. I'm not seeking to put further doubts in my readers' minds than are already there. But what I do seek to do is to name and explore the vivid feelings of betrayal, despair, 'lost-ness', shame, fear, sorrow and profound, perhaps total, abandonment that Christ experiences in his Passion, and at least hint at the ways these feelings are mirrored in the lives of my readers. The cross is the gospel – but it's not the whole of the gospel. This is what the worshipper rediscovers every Holy Week. If a person goes to church on Good Friday and doesn't return on Easter Day, they may expect to find themself in an unresolved state of turmoil, confusion and dismay. If a person appears at church on Easter Day without having been present on Good Friday, they may expect to sense they're in the midst of relief for which they knew not the preceding anxiety, joy for which they shared not the foregoing terror, plenitude for which they perceived not the former scarcity.

But the result of the way I strive to resist any suggestion that the cross, while painful and ghastly, was part of a Plan and therefore, ultimately, fine, is that this is a book not just about how the cross addresses the greatest challenges to the Christian faith, but about how it does so by redescribing how salvation comes about. Only when we recognize that an easy narration of the cross is finished, and our faith is hanging by a thread, can we appreciate how the cross represents our salvation.

In this book I explore six questions that I believe the cross asks us – all of which are different versions of the same question. In each case I believe the cross leaves us hanging by a thread. I begin with the question of story and history. There's no use pretending we have any access to the cross except through the accounts the Gospels give us. And those accounts are subject to the same limitations and scrutiny as any historical documents: they reflect the bias of their authors, they're locked in the era in which they were written, they're a restricted subjective view rather than an unlimited objective one. So this is the place to begin: we have to enjoy, to relish being bearers of a story, rather than desperately trying to make a story tell us things no story can. If we want to turn the cross into a conventional history, our faith will be left hanging by a thread; instead, we need to discover what it means for God to enter into our story, and to be moved to enter into God's story.

I then move to the question of trust. Faith is fundamentally about trust. Trust isn't the opposite of knowledge, for that presupposes a false notion of knowledge. Knowledge isn't certainty: it's more like apprehension of an array of dots that one's in the habit of connecting together, rather as stargazers join together stars into constellations. The dots are there, but the joining is largely convention. The difference between convention and faith isn't as great as is often supposed. Nonetheless trust is the explicit recognition of relying on what cannot be known – particularly as experienced in interpersonal relations. This human level has always been important: but it has become especially so in recent decades in the West, as acceptance of institutions and hierarchies has been challenged, and authority-structures have been dismantled. What remains is interpersonal trust: but the cross deals such trust a savage blow.

The third question is that of mortality. The simplest description of the conventional portrayal of the cross is that it is the way God overcomes the burden of sin and the curse of death. In John 11 Jesus says, 'I am the resurrection and the life. Those who believe in me, even though they die, will live, and everyone who lives and believes in me will never die.' But plenty of people have lived and believed in Jesus – and nonetheless died. Does death expose existence, as Macbeth supposed, as no more than 'a walking shadow, a poor player/That struts and frets his hour upon the stage/ And then is heard no more'? Is life simply 'a tale/Told by an idiot, full of sound and fury,/Signifying nothing'? If so, faith is a curious sideshow on a fundamentally futile circus. But again, that question can't be addressed by changing the subject or diverting attention to something urgent or entertaining. The question is at the heart of the cross.

The fourth question is, consequently, purpose. I begin with story, because it's story that gives us the cross in the first place. I then move to trust and death, because they are the two most visceral issues that face human beings. But there are two less pressing, but equally important questions to address. The first is meaning and purpose. This is the moment to widen the lens from the intensity of human experience. I do so in two ways, by looking at the earth's place in the universe of time and space, and by considering humanity's place in a Darwinian notion of evolution. These are perhaps the two greatest challenges to the self-importance and self-centredness of any human story. They jeopardize the validity not just of Christianity, but of most alternative human narratives. As elsewhere, I want not to wince as they leave faith hanging by a thread, but to examine that thread in the light of the cross and find it none other than the way to life and peace.

The fifth question, more than the others, concerns social location. It's about power, and about the way knowledge and influence and faith are shaped – and in the view of some, determined – in terms of power relations. Questions about the cross are not the same for everybody: they differ depending on your present and historic connection to sources and uses of power. This can lead to hopeful activism or angry cynicism. But it's so much in the contemporary imagination that one can't consider the cross without reflecting on how power works, and whether its dynamics dominate, undermine, or are subverted by faith.

The final question, that of love, intentionally circles us back to the opening two questions – story and trust, against the backdrop of the third question, death. Elsewhere I've argued that 'with' is the most important word in theology. Here I illustrate that assertion in narrative form, in ways that touch also on meaning and to a lesser degree on power. The last question is designed to draw together the insights of all the foregoing questions and explorations. It's facile to move too quickly to talk of love without considering the five questions that precede it; but absurd to try to explore the cross without attempting to fathom what wondrous love is this. By the end, the hope is that the reader joins the words of Samuel Crossman, and resolves: Here might I stay and sing.

The last chapter – the seventh candle – doesn't seek to answer a question: it attempts to stay and sing in the place created by the sixth chapter. Too many books or arguments about the truth of faith or the nature of salvation end where you want them to start – make a case, but stop when that case has been made. Here I try to stay still for a while, and dwell in the implications of what the sixth question has led us to. I've the given the seventh chapter the same title as the first chapter, so as to show that the argument ends where it begins. It is, in T. S. Eliot's celebrated words in 'Little Gidding', 'to arrive where we started/And know the place for the first time'. Rather like the six days of creation, which end with the sabbath, that contemplates and completes the six days, this short book is taken up with six questions, and concludes with a chapter of dwelling, that seeks to amplify and embody the proposals that forego it.

1

Story

The Bible presents itself as a story of everything: Genesis begins with the words, 'In the beginning when God created the heavens and the earth', and John's Gospel echoes that cosmic scope by starting with, 'In the beginning was the Word'. But with the failures of Adam, Cain and Noah, the Bible becomes a story of how God chose one people, Abraham and his descendants, the twelve tribes of Jacob. What began as a wide-canvas epic becomes a lyric tale of God's love for Israel, whose destiny continually hangs by a thread. Israel is starved in Canaan, enslaved in Egypt, lost in the wilderness, outnumbered in the Promised Land, leaderless in the time of the Judges, overrun by the Assyrians and the Chaldeans, exiled in Babylon, and almost obliterated by the scheming Haman in Susa. At every stage everybody wonders, and usually somebody says, 'God has abandoned us' – and who can blame them for imagining so?

At the centre of the Old Testament is the covenant that God makes with Moses on Mt Sinai. The story of the Old Testament is of how that covenant came to be made and of whether that covenant will survive the tragedies and tribulations of Israel's faithfulness and folly. Perhaps the crucial moment in that unfolding drama comes in Babylon, when Israel reflects back on the thousand or so years since the covenant, and realizes it's as close to God in exile as it ever was in the Promised Land. The prophet Hosea tells this story in all its simplicity and poignancy. 'When Israel was a child,' God says in Hosea 11, 'I loved him … I led them with cords of human kindness, with bands of love. I was to them like those who lift infants to their cheeks … The more I called them, the more they went from me … How can I hand you over, O Israel? I will not execute my fierce anger … I will not come in wrath … I will return them to their homes.' Here we see God's side of the story.

All of this shapes how we understand the cross. The Gospels present Jesus as the embodiment of the covenant, utterly Israel and utterly God. Jesus re-enacts the great events of Israel's history; being baptized at the Jordan to reflect Joshua entering the Promised Land across the Jordan, spending 40 days in the wilderness to mirror Israel's 40 years, calling twelve disciples to echo Israel's twelve tribes, delivering a sermon on the mount to imitate Moses' time with God on Mt Sinai, right up until his body is destroyed on the cross like Israel's temple was destroyed by the Chaldeans. At the same time the rejection of Jesus by the scribes and Pharisees and Sanhedrin is presented as the final among Israel's long list of failures to honour the covenant. And yet, just as Israel was closer to God in exile than ever elsewhere, so we are closer to God at the moment of Jesus' crucifixion, his ultimate exile from God and from us, than at any other moment.

Jesus assumes the mantle of Israel, suffering for all Israel's sins, and finally achieving what the temple was there to do – make good God's relationship with Israel through repentance embodied in sacrifice. But Jesus also thereby makes a new covenant, not just with Israel, but with all humankind. This is the great gift of St Paul, who in his life and his letters demonstrates how forgiveness and eternal life are extended to all who believe.

And this is where the problem arises. We could call it one problem with three manifestations. The problem we can call history – or to put it more aptly, what happens when story meets history. The first manifestation of the problem is a moral one. In order to explain why God opened the covenant up to Gentiles, the Church started to tell a terrible story of what was wrong with the Jews. And that led to centuries of persecution and culminated in the Holocaust. That legacy of persecution is so damaging that it threatens to leave the moral credibility of Christianity hanging by a thread. But it has more subtle aspects. It's fashionable in some congregations to express misgivings about conventional doctrines of the atonement that suggest Jesus died as a sacrificial victim in our place, or took the world's sins on his back, or that portray Jesus as a conquering hero destroying death and parading down the heavenly way. But notice that all of these atonement theories have one thing in common: they attempt to tell the story of God in a manner that airbrushes out the Jews altogether. The scar of the Church's conscience about the Jews isn't limited to historical oppression: it's riven through conventional doctrine too.

The second manifestation of what happens when story meets history is a factual one. What do we do when textual scholars and archaeologists cast serious doubts on whether some crucial parts of the story measure up to historical scrutiny? If there wasn't, say, an Abraham, or if there's no evidence of an exodus – if Haman's threat in the book of Esther to exterminate the Jews is a made-up fable? What do we make of the Bible, if important elements may never really have happened? When story becomes 'just a story'? Is our heritage hanging by a thread?

And the third dimension of history is a philosophical one. Even if one grants that the most significant parts of the story do indeed match with the historical record, how can one event, that happened once in one place, have significance for the meaning of everything, everywhere? As one eighteenth-century philosopher put it, how can accidental truths of history become the proof of necessary truths of reason? Isn't there a yawning chasm between faith, that holds great store by particular events and people, and history, that derives conclusions from universal phenomena? Doesn't this leave faith hanging by a thread?

Much thought has been put into rescuing Christianity from the dangling thread of history that these three dimensions bring about. When we look at the cross, we see the agony and the isolation of Christ, but to believe it's all in vain, that it's pointless to imagine one moment of sacrifice can represent everything or change anything – that makes the agony all the more excruciating. How can we keep hold of the tiny thread of faith in the face of the dismantling tendency of history?

Charles Dickens' novel *A Tale of Two Cities* tells of two men who look extraordinarily alike. One is Charles Darnay, a French aristocrat whose relatives have caused untold suffering to the common people in the decades prior to the French Revolution. He marries the winsome Lucie, even though both realize that his family have caused her terrible grief, including her father's long imprisonment. The other man is Sydney Carton, an alcoholic and depressive English barrister, who also loves Lucie, but fails to win her hand. At the climax of the novel, Charles, who returns to Paris, is arrested and faces the guillotine. But Sydney, playing on the resemblance between the two, in love of Lucie and desire for once to make something worthy of his life, drugs Charles and goes to the guillotine in his place, saying, 'It is a far, far better thing that I do, than I have ever done; it is a far, far better rest I go to than I have ever known.'

What Sydney's gesture shows us is that Jesus' cross may be inseparable from his place in Israel's story; but that all of us can take up our cross and follow him. We can't make sense of Jesus detached from God's covenant with Israel; but we can imitate Jesus in the way we make and renew our covenants with one another. We can't insert ourselves in the turbulent events of first-century Jerusalem; but we can allow ourselves to be enfolded by God's story, transformed by Jesus' sacrifice, and moved to walk in his steps. If left to our intellect alone, we will constantly find reasons why our connection to a faraway figure in a faraway country at a faraway time moves little, matters less, and means nothing. But, like Sydney Carton, we each face moments in our existence when we have the chance to say or do something that shows what we believe life is for, existence is about, and truth is made of. Jesus' sacrificial death is that far, far better thing. Our connection to it may seem, for much of our life, to hang by a thread. But when we face the moment of truth, we come face to face with the cross. And we discover that, hanging by the thread, is none other than Jesus.

2

Trust

In the face of the onslaught of critical historical and scientific analyses in the eighteenth and nineteenth centuries, Christianity turned inward. The test of truth became not so much 'Did this happen?' or 'Can it be proven?' but 'Has it changed my life?' and 'Does it make me feel close to God?'

In 1995 the Committee on Standards in Public Life issued what are known as the Nolan Principles for guiding those in public office. They are Selflessness, Integrity, Objectivity, Accountability, Openness, Honesty and Leadership. It was a commendable attempt to elucidate what authority involves today. The trouble is, that ship sailed a long time ago. Authority is tied to an extensive and stable network of relationships and a hierarchy of duties and responsibilities. The TV series *Downton Abbey* was almost entirely made up of adventures that involved some trespass of these expectations; almost every plot was resolved by the imaginative reassertion of the hierarchy of duty. People are perpetually suspicious of authority, be it police, teachers, clergy or politicians, not simply because of egregious personal failures, but because our culture has largely repudiated the whole idea of hierarchical roles and relationships. Once we may have not have liked authority figures, but we still trusted them; today we may like them, but we don't trust them.

A similar change has taken place in relation to community. Almost everyone regards community as a good word – a place of stability, trust, shared values, joint efforts and abiding respect. But I wonder how many people reading these words are still living in the neighbourhood in which they grew up. Very few, I'm guessing. And how many are sad about that? Not that many, I'd imagine. Why? Because community may offer trust, but that trust comes at a price of indelible prejudice, small-mindedness, long memories for things you'd prefer to be forgotten, resistance to change, and the death of ambition. You go back to your home town and suddenly you feel infantilized: everyone expects you to have pigtails and wear short trousers. We say we want community, and the trust that comes with never locking our doors; but we make social choices that suggest the opposite. And for good reasons.

So that means we place a colossal weight of expectation on intimate relationships to bear the whole burden of trust that once used to be shared across authority structures and local communities. I often wonder how it is that for all our tolerance about sexuality and our dismantling of many time-honoured taboos, almost everyone agrees that betrayal in a relationship is a terrible thing. I think the reason is that when we've stopped believing in almost everything, the romantic idea that two people can be so in love that it can last for ever is one of the few sacred things society still holds dear. But our sense of intimate trust isn't restricted to sexual partnership. Take the acronym BFF. Instagram would die out tomorrow if we couldn't declare one another Best Friends Forever. There'd be no teenage television if we abandoned the plotline about the person you thought was your friend turning out nasty and then making up. In short, we've domesticated trust, instrumentalized most of the relationships of the market or the workplace, and evacuated public life of mutual responsibility.

All of which makes the passion narrative horrifying reading. On Palm Sunday everyone wants to be Jesus' friend. The tidal wave of popularity that has on occasion looked like carrying Jesus to national prominence lifts him high on a crest of the palm branches and cloaks and hallelujahs. But a few days later the same crowd has turned sour and their eyes have turned to hatred as they screech 'Crucify!' You can't trust a crowd. You can't place your faith in popularity. It blows with the wind.

But what about Jesus' nearest and dearest? One of the twelve, Judas, can't bear the way things are going. What's his problem? Is it that he believes Jesus has everything but is tossing it away, just like the woman who tossed away a wealth of perfume by using it to wash Jesus' feet? Is it that he wakes up and realizes he's backed the wrong horse, and violent confrontation is the only way to displace the Romans? Is it that he envies Jesus and aches to get the limelight himself? Or does he think he knows better than

Jesus and wants to force Jesus to defeat the Romans by triggering a dramatic showdown? We'll never know. But at the most intimate moment of friendship, the Last Supper, Judas and Jesus dip their bread together – before Judas runs out to give the game away. It's a fundamental betrayal: deliberate, planned, devastating. And what of the other disciples? They go to Gethsemane, Jesus asks three of them to watch while he prays, and they nod off, away with the fairies, stashing zeds, not once, not twice – but three times. The spirit is willing but the flesh is weak. That's the kindest possible interpretation.

Then the soldiers arrive and the disciples scarper. So much for all their promises to be by Jesus' side until kingdom come. When the going gets tough the tough get lost. And all roll over till there's one left. Peter. In the courtyard, cock-a-doodle-doo. Not once, not twice, but three times. This isn't flaky Judas or soon-to-be-doubting Thomas. This is Peter, the rock, the one with the keys of the kingdom of heaven, the first pope, the Church's one foundation.

What a scene of devastation. Don't let the fact that you know the story so well allow you to ignore how catastrophic this is. We have a script half-written in our heads: Jesus is misunderstood by the masses, double-crossed by the authorities, cynically disposed of by the Romans – but his tight-knit band of brothers, his beloved disciples, these happy few, who lived that day and saw old age, would yearly on the vigil feast their neighbours; those that outlived that day, and came safe home, would stand a-tip-toe when that day was named. And those who had been a-bed would think themselves accursed they were not there, because these household names would forever be celebrated for the wonder that togetherness, and comradeship, and unflinching bonds of loyalty could achieve. That's the story, straight out of Henry V, we so want to believe – that arbitrary duty and outdated responsibility are vanquished, but true commitment, profound trust and eyeball-to-eyeball loyalty conquer everything.

But it turns out that story's in tatters. Our trust in human goodness, in the power of love and best friends for ever and manly handshakes and undying commitment is practically spent. It's hanging by a thread. You know that winsome phrase, 'Never doubt that a small group of thoughtful, committed citizens can change the world; indeed, it's the only thing that ever has.' It sums up our contemporary conviction that institutions and authority are bunk but the power of trust and loyalty and commitment can achieve anything. Well, whoever coined that phrase hadn't read the Passion narrative for a while. The Passion story tells how a small group of thoughtful, committed citizens totally disintegrated into betrayal, snoring, flight and denial. It's as if Jesus anticipated our contemporary faith in personal relationships and said, 'Don't be so sentimental. You're loading on to personal trust a burden it can't bear: look at what the disciples are really like. What makes you think you're any different?'

The first of the great five points of Calvinist doctrine is the notion of total depravity. Total depravity doesn't mean we human beings are utterly evil: it simply means we're incapable of doing good. Such good that we appear to do is flawed in both its intention and its action. What looks like altruism is in fact cleverly-disguised egocentrism. As the prayer of confession puts it, 'We have left undone those things which we ought to have done; and we have done those things which we ought not to have done; and there is no health in us.' Our trust in ourselves is hanging by a thread.

But it's not as simple as that. Humanity is also capable of grace and kindness beyond our imagination. And that goodness is visible in the Holy Week story too. A woman anoints Jesus' feet and prepares him for burial. Simon of Cyrene carries Christ's burden. The women gather at the cross. Joseph of Arimathaea steps forward to provide a tomb. There's excitement, noble service, sacrificial love, humble devotion. Humanity doesn't just touch the depths of depravity; it reaches the heights of glory. That's what makes the story so poignant – so painful. There's still that tiny thread of grace. It would be so much simpler if we could simply say we were all good or all bad. As John Cleese said, 'It's not the despair I can't stand. It's the hope.' Hanging by a thread.

On the night of 6 March 1987, a cross-channel sea ferry carrying 500 people sank in the Belgian port of Zeebrugge, 90 seconds after leaving harbour. The assistant boatswain had fallen asleep and failed to close the bow doors. The first officer hadn't been present to check they were closed, and the boatswain had seen they were open but chose not to close them because it wasn't his job. So water gushed into the open doors and the ship capsized, with the loss of nearly 200 lives. Later inquiries revealed culpability and complacency at every level of management. Almost every dimension of human folly, fragility and depravity contributed to the disaster. It was like the Passion narrative all over again.

And yet assistant bank manager Andrew Parker, a passenger on the ferry that night, did a quite extraordinary thing. He saw two metal barriers, and, below, in the gap between them, he saw onrushing water. Behind him were dozens of people. So he held on to one barrier with his fists and the other with his ankles, and made his own body into a human bridge by stretching between the two barriers. Some 20 terrified people, including his own wife and daughter, climbed over him to safety. How he found the courage and strength, how he still was rescued after laying down his life for so many, no one could say. But there was no doubt that in that disaster the world could see both the depths of human failure and the heights of human aspiration.

We approach the Passion story assuming God is just like us – liable to terrible and merciless wrath, but also capable of amazing grace. But that's not what the Passion tells us. We're a mixture of good and bad, but God is good all the way down, all the time, all the way beyond for ever and back. Holy Week is the story of what happens when our mixed-up lives come in touching distance of a goodness that goes beyond for ever, and what happens to that goodness – that goodness –and what happens to us.

The Passion of Christ shows us that Jesus is stretched out between heaven and earth, hanging by a thread between the limitless possibilities of human goodness and the fathomless horror of human depravity. Jesus' body is stretched out, like Andrew Parker's body, between the metal barrier of human folly and the metal barrier of God's grace. Jesus' body is stretched out like a violin string between the two. And the name we give that agonizing stretching-out is the cross. If we were all good, it wouldn't be so poignant. If we were all bad, it wouldn't be so painful. We're still God's creation, we're still God's beloved, so we're worth saving; but we're still cowardly, cruel and crooked, so the saving costs God everything. Jesus is the hanging thread, the violin string stretched out between heaven and earth.

And the music played on that string is what we call the gospel.

3
Life

When philosophers contemplate all things, they traditionally start with the question, 'Why is there something rather than nothing?' It's clearly a fundamental question. It points to the great mystery of existence, which is that 'something'. But it's almost too big to contemplate, both because 'something' seems an inadequate term to indicate the reality of all creation, and because it's hard to get your head round the notion of 'nothing'. It's challenging because we take existence for granted, and to say 'Why is there something rather than nothing?' is to change the default, the normal, to nothing. Rather than see only deficit, and be stuck in resentment, complaint and disappointment about our lot, setting the default to nothing can only make us grateful, and fill us with awe at the tiniest detail of creation. Why *is* there something rather than nothing? And since there is, will there always be?

Helpful as this question is, I think there's a related question that feels closer to home. Given the wonder and complexity of life, how can there be death? The intricate structure and workings of even the tiniest creature are marvellous beyond words; breathing and eating produce strength and energy, growth and movement, reproduction is dazzling in its subtlety and tenderness, and each new creature somehow already knows or soon learns how to make its way in the world. When it comes to human beings, the complexity and subtlety and wonder are multiplied many times over. You see a tiny baby, and the eye already sees and blinks, the nose can smell, the teeny fingers are all there, and language hasn't developed but the voice is already loud and clear. From then on relationship and creativity and appetite and imagination only expand, and potential seems limitless.

But we die. It all comes to an end. We live most of our lives in more or less total denial of this fact. We make ourselves so busy, focus on matters in hand so closely, fill every idle moment with entertainment or distraction, that we block out our mortality; even when we confront death, in movie catastrophe or gruesome newsflash, in random accident, hospital ward or funeral parlour, even when death eats up the most precious people in our lives, we still perpetuate the smokescreen that this will not happen to us. Doubtless the world is a dangerous place, but through a mixture of planning, medicine, prayer and luck, we might just get out of it alive. The most absurd expression in the language is, 'Why me?' If you do the maths, you don't find a lot of people who escape death; and in the light of eternity, you wouldn't think a couple of dozen years of life either way counted for a great deal; but we still say 'Why me?', disclosing, as we do so, that we deep down thought we could cheat death if we played our cards right.

When we say the word 'life' we mean a number of related but not identical things. Life means bare life, not dying, perhaps in the last throes but nonetheless breathing, heart-beating, still on our side of the great divide. Life also means really living, unconstrained, free, in our prime, creative, flourishing, vibrant. More precisely, life means a time well-lived, capacities extended to the utmost, athleticism, intelligence, virtue, artistry, invention that dazzle and stretch the possibility of planet and species. More generally, life can mean the sustenance of the ecosphere, all that's put in threat by climate change and environmental depredation. And ultimately life means existence itself, where we started, why there's something and not nothing, and what it means for that something to abide and not lapse into nothing.

When we read about Peter's confrontation with Jesus on the road to Caesarea Philippi, we tend to think how stupid Peter was, how slow to get it, how fixated he was on the notion of a military triumphalist messiah. But consider everything I've just said about life. And consider that, in his own terms, Peter knew all that. And here was Jesus, who did so many new things and said so many true things. And Peter thought, naturally enough, 'This is the one who is going to give us life, real life, not the kind that blossoms and flourishes then withers and perishes, but everlasting life, without fear, pain, and despair.' So imagine his consternation when Jesus says, 'The Son of Man must undergo great suffering, and be rejected by the elders, the chief priests, and the scribes, and be killed.' It's devastating.

It's like the scene in the war movie when the insurgents are pouring through the jungle towards the river and suddenly the last bridge is blown up and they're left marooned for ever on the far side of nowhere. Jesus is that bridge from fragile life to eternal life, and his words to Peter are like the detonator that destroys the last hope.

We've seen in the first two chapters that Jesus' death is the disastrous culmination of Israel's story and that the disciples' betrayal and denial is the most damaging possible indictment of our hope that personal relationships can withstand the ravages of our loss of trust in anyone and anything. Now we face the third challenge of the cross. We find that life itself, something rather than nothing, not just our own lives but the existence of all things, is hanging by a thread.

The traditional way to face this challenge is to say that on the cross Jesus somehow stepped out of his naked, suffocating, bleeding body and became some kind of a warrior that defeated death. Some of the theologians of the early centuries suggested that Adam and Eve had traded humanity to Satan, and that God therefore owed Satan a ransom. God gave Satan Christ, satisfying the ransom, so the grip of death was released; but death couldn't hold Jesus so Satan lost on all counts. While widely influential, this theory makes God a debtor and a deceiver. Beyond that, it distorts the humanity and tenderness of Jesus' life as recorded in the Gospels into a spectacular melodrama.

The alternative historical way to portray the crucifixion is to assume that death is a result of sin, and that the only way humanity could be reconciled with God is by humanity making a consummate sacrifice. Since the sin was too great for a human sacrifice to be enough, God provided, in the form of Jesus, a sufficient yet also human sacrifice, thus achieving reconciliation and forever disarming the power of sin. The fruits of that reconciliation are inherited by all who believe. This presents a confusing picture of God, as one who loves us but is either unwilling or unable to forgive us without requiring dreadful suffering, and is all-powerful yet subject to an elaborate punitive scheme of law. Again this seems out of step with the way Jesus is portrayed in the Gospels. Beyond that, it's so focused on sin it still seems to leave death as scary as ever.

I've already referred to the problem that most of the Church's attempts to make meaning out of Jesus' death are subtle ways of airbrushing the Jews out of the Christian story. The two theories I just mentioned both exhibit that tendency. But there's something more profoundly wrong with such theories. And that is, they both take Peter's side of the dispute at Caesarea Philippi. That's to say, they're both trying to make Jesus' death somehow OK, part of a plan, all orchestrated and comprehensible and appropriate. And that sanitizes the horror of this day. This is the day when the highest political authority washed its hands, the exalted religious leaders connived and manipulated, the common people turned accusers and haters, the circle of close friends fled, the right-hand man betrayed, the self-styled best friend forever denied. This is as awful as it gets, for faith, government, friendship, loyalty, love. It's not

Good Friday. It's terrible Friday, the worst day of all time, when we see the absolute horror of who we are, and the absolute finality of death, not just for the clumsy, the fragile and the foolish, like us, but even for our greatest hope, the good, the beautiful, the true – Jesus.

But the cross is not just the moment when we see the truth of who we are. It's also the moment when we see the truth of who God is. After Jesus' conversation with Peter at Caesarea Philippi, he turns to the crowd and says, 'If any want to become my followers, let them deny themselves and take up their cross and follow me.' In other words, the cross is the inevitable fate of those who face the evil, sin and death of the world with goodness, courage and love. Jesus isn't going to a lonely place where we can't join him for a pistols-at-dawn face-off with death on a special commission from the Father. He's forging a path that we can follow. The closer we stay to him, the nearer we come to life.

He goes on to say, 'Those who want to save their life will lose it, and those who lose their life for my sake, and for the sake of the gospel, will save it.' You can't cling on to life. It'll sooner or later slip through your hands. Let go of life. You can't keep it. Instead, hold on to Jesus. Let him take you by the hand and lead you through the streets of suffering, pain, hardship and death. He'll show you something better than life. Jesus didn't want to die. He was frightened just as you and I are. But he walked towards Jerusalem and he walked towards Calvary because he was crafting a path for us through death to something better than life. The alternative to that something is nothing. And the only way towards that something is to take his hand, to reel in that thread, so we are no longer hanging on to life by a thread, but holding on to Jesus.

In 1932 as Thomas Dorsey was leading a service at the Ebenezer Baptist Church in Chicago, a man came on to the platform and handed him a telegram that said, 'Your wife Nettie has died giving birth.' He rushed home, only to find the baby also died shortly afterwards. Thomas faced his own crucifixion. He was hanging on to faith, and sanity, by a thread. Sitting in a friend's house a few days later, he experienced a peace the world cannot give. He began to sing words that came from the mouth of the Holy Spirit. 'Precious Lord, take my hand, Lead me on, let me stand, I am tired, I am weak, I am worn; Through the storm, through the night, Lead me on to the light: Take my hand, precious Lord, Lead me home.'

There's no way to avoid death. You can't spend eternity hanging by a thread. Jesus went to the cross, and made his way through death to something beyond life. Let him take your hand, tired, weak and worn, and his journey will be yours too.

4

Purpose

Not long ago I went back to my old school for the first time in 30 years. I sat in a classroom with a bunch of sixth-formers and we talked about philosophy and ethics. It was only much later, after coming back to London, that I realized what was special about that classroom. It was there on a battered old contraption that showed mini-reels of film, that as a twelve-year-old I watched an eight-minute spool called *Cosmic Zoom*.

That mini-movie was probably the most memorable moment in my whole time at school. It starts with a view of a boy rowing his black labrador in a boat on the Ottawa River in Canada. The image quickly pans out, and you see the river from high above, then a mile high, then on and on where you can see the earth, then the moon, then you keep widening the lens past the Solar System, the Milky Way and ultimately the far reaches of the universe. Then the camera stops, and begins to zoom back through every stage, eventually reaching the boy on the boat. But it doesn't stop there. It keeps zooming in, on the boy's hand, and on a mosquito perched there. It zeroes down into the insect's proboscis and on into each tiny element until it reaches an atomic nucleus. Then it reverses again up to a same-sight view of the boy rowing the boat.

I was no instinctive scientist, I can assure you: so the idea of condensing everything I needed to know about physics, chemistry and biology into a rapid eight minutes appealed to me a lot. But what really captivated me was the more philosophical argument the film subtly communicated. It takes four minutes to pan out and survey the wide universe beyond, and four minutes to delve in and discover the tiny world within. In other words, human beings are the measure of all things. The level of complexity inside them is equivalent to the level of complexity outside them. You don't have to look into the early chapters of Genesis; here, in the gospel of high school science, is just as bold a statement of faith: humankind is the crown of creation, the keystone of the triumphal arch.

That becomes important when you begin to think about the two great scientific challenges of the modern era. The first is cosmology. Cosmology explores the origin, evolution and ultimate fate of the universe. Copernicus, Kepler and Galileo pointed out that the earth wasn't the centre of the universe – it circled the sun. Newton showed that earth and the heavens obey the same laws of physics. Einstein's discoveries led to the conclusion that the universe was not static but expanding, and Lemaître proposed the Big Bang theory about the universe's origins. Many cosmologists believe that what expands will one day contract, and thus produce an ultimate Big Crunch resulting in a black hole or a new Big Bang. The issue here is not just space but time. Not long ago it was announced that the universe was 13.8 billion years old. Happy birthday. But that puts life in perspective. It's said that if cosmic history were mapped onto a football pitch, all of human existence would fit onto a human hand.

The other great challenge comes from evolutionary biology. This starts from the conviction that the diversity of life was not created as such but that all life on earth started from a single source. Darwin's two great principles were that mutation happened randomly, and that mutation caused diversification and competition in a process known as the survival of the fittest.

Cosmology and evolutionary biology are usually portrayed as the great antagonists of Christianity, although the notion of a God who put the earth at the centre of the universe, and created each animal in exactly its present form, let alone a Bible that was intended to be a science textbook, are ideas most Christians left behind a long time ago. More interesting is to note how profoundly cosmology and evolutionary biology challenge a conventional secular understanding of human worth, as expressed in the eight-minute film *Cosmic Zoom*. In short, the two academic disciplines offer the withering assumptions that on the one hand the universe isn't coming from or going anywhere in particular, and the earth is nothing special amidst it all, and on the other hand that life on earth is equally purposeless and without especial origin or destiny, while in evolution's chaotic and unpredictable trajectory there's no privileged place for humankind either.

All of which leaves any sense of meaning or purpose in existence hanging by a thread. It locates Jesus' death in an obscure backwater of the universe, as a member of a self-important but not indispensable species, as a representative of a self-absorbed but ultimately peripheral race, at a relatively uninteresting juncture in planetary history. It's not just a jungle-dweller of 3,000 years ago, unaware of the rest of the planet; it's not just the imprisoned slave under a tyrannical regime, languishing in a forgotten cell; it's not just the contemporary Reggie Perrin, driven to distraction by the pointlessness of his career at Sunshine Desserts: everyone, it seems, has a meaningless, purposeless existence – even Jesus. Any shape, goal or direction of existence is hanging by a thread.

There are two ways to come to terms with this. The first is to be defensive – to say it's impossible to live without a sense of purpose, absurd to imagine a universe coming into being without a reason, harder to conceive of purposelessness in the abstract than meaning in the concrete. Even those who claim to have no purpose make meanings to live by. The geneticist J. B. S. Haldane said a sense of ultimate purpose 'is like a mistress to the biologist; he dare not be seen with her in public but cannot live without her.' But these arguments are in the end useless, because it's a long way from saying people need meaning, to any sense that those meanings are true.

Instead we need to stop trying to shout into the whirlwind. The significance of Christ's agonizing death on the cross isn't that it's a knockdown outright winner for most meaningful moment in the history of the universe. Quite the opposite. It's squalid, shameful, invisible and pointless. The people who put a massive Christ figure, with arms stretched wide, looming over the city of Rio de Janeiro, got it all wrong. Jesus dies as he's born, on the edge, out of the limelight, an afterthought, a reject, pushed into the gutter. Rather than make the cross implausible, the work of cosmologists and evolutionary biologists in dismantling meaning structures actually enhances the poignancy of the crucifixion. God is among us, not as a commanding statue on the plinth of creation, not as a climax of a compelling story, but as a pointless death among a defeated people in a ravaged nation.

I remember once hearing an evangelist claim that Christ died deliberately at a crucial moment in the expansion of the Roman Empire at a crossroads location between east and west and north and south, so the message of Christianity could soon go far and wide to the ends of the earth. But that's completely to miss the point. That's to shout into the whirlwind, to try to make God bigger than the universe and more powerful than the mutations of evolution. It's to miss Christ's humility altogether.

One twentieth-century French poet coined a resonant phrase. 'There is another world,' he said, 'but it's inside this one.' Think about what that means in relation to Pilate's question, 'What is truth?', or what it says about our exploration of meaning and purpose in the wake of cosmology and evolutionary biology. The truth doesn't lie in the grand design or the unshakeable plan. It lies in going inside what's in front of you, going deeper, looking into the heart of things.

I knew a family who had an 18-month old child who caused havoc around the house by pushing his little toy sit-on bus and crashing it into the furniture. The family were always busy and it took them longer than most to realize that one Christmas some significant things were going missing. They considered theft, they wondered if they were losing the plot, and they even looked under the cabinets to see if the active toddler had knocked things off with his crashing bus and they'd fallen under something. Finally they saw the toddler open the lid of the bus, and inside they saw the four missing things: his favourite toy, the TV remote control, his dad's mobile phone and the baby Jesus from the nativity set. He somehow knew what made the household tick. The secret was not to look around – but to look inside.

On the cross Jesus goes to the heart of it all. He goes inside sin, inside death, inside suffering, pain, rejection, hurt, violence, hunger, agony, evil. He goes inside them all. It's not part of an orchestrated plan, or a contrived trick, or a legal theory. He enters the heart of darkness, the black hole of horror, the vortex of meaninglessness. And if we're to respond to the cross, we're not to treat it as some kind of device, some instrument or technique in a preordained master-plan. We respond to Jesus' crucified body by entering into the heart of that body, looking into the soul of that suffering figure, finding the other world that's inside this one. The crucified God isn't a trick, or a device, or a pathetic attempt to do something big and meaningful. It's an acceptance of the horror and pointlessness of existence, and a willingness to go inside existence, to zoom down into the interior of reality, and be unflinching in whatever is discovered there.

And here's the mystery. Jesus goes deep into the heart of things, within the horror and sin and death and dismay, beneath the purposeless meaninglessness of existence. Jesus is that toddler working his way around the cosmological house with his toy bus. And when we see his heart on the cross and open up the lid of his toy bus, what we see there is the surprise, mystery and miracle of the gospel. What we see there is us.

5
Power

Perhaps unsurprisingly, the idea that existence is meaningless hasn't proved that popular even among the class of people that delve into cosmology and evolutionary biology. On the level of everyday life, it's still the case that for most of the world's population, the greater part of every day is spent seeking survival, by the basic standards of food, water, clothing, shelter and physical security. On the level of the more comfortable and relatively affluent, many people's lives are dominated by the struggle for advantage, profit, favour and pleasure. As a result, the consensus seems to be not that existence is meaningless, but that its shape is determined by a select few, whose will is seldom benevolent. In other words, we're obsessed by power.

The Church's cultured despisers, including the so-called new atheists, are full of biological and other scientific criticisms of faith; but the real heat of the anger is a moral one. They deeply resent the Church's power. They see the damage religion has done politically in war and personally in disordered hearts, minds and relationships. They see the word 'God' as an emotive way to manipulate people's actions, commitments, and lives.

The eighteenth-century Enlightenment was, more than anything else, an attempt to free the human mind from the backward and controlling influence of the Church. Since then a cascade of thinkers has burst forth, each with their own account of power and narrative of how it's been suppressed, manipulated or restricted. Each of these accounts seems so all-encompassing that there's nothing it can't explain: and that includes the cross. So Karl Marx sees a fundamental class struggle between owners and labourers: for him Jesus' death is simply the assertion of power by the ruling class against a person that advanced the claims of the people. It's a class war, religious war and a war of independence, and Jesus is crushed along with the thousands of rebels the Romans crucified.

Friedrich Nietzsche sees Jesus as a noble figure but Christianity as offering a calamitous indulgence of weakness and vulnerability. The cross is problematic not so much for Jesus' suffering but for the way that suffering has been glorified in subsequent devotion. For Sigmund Freud the primal themes are the child's discovery of the urge to destroy, an urge that extends even to sources of deepest sustenance, notably the mother. Jesus' crucifixion and resurrection are therefore a myth; that is, an enacted story of how we discover our own destructiveness and the goodness and resilience and love of the other whom we long to destroy. For Michel Foucault crucifixion is at the same time the way the Roman Empire demonstrated that its peoples were fundamentally powerless slaves, and the way an absolute God declares, as in the story of Abraham and Isaac, that there are no limits to the obedience that can be demanded of creaturely beings.

In case this seems no more than a litany of dead white men, these are the figures people constantly draw on today when they configure religion and society as the playing fields of power. So for example, feminists draw on Nietzsche and Foucault when listening to the testimony of women experiencing domestic violence, criticizing the pastoral advice to enter into and share the sufferings of Christ. Liberation theologians draw on Marx to identify the struggle of the poor in South America with Jesus' walk to the cross. Spiritual directors and counsellors draw on Freud when they help a person recognize how readily they push away the attention of those they most dearly love.

What the accounts of Marx and Nietzsche and Freud and Foucault have in common, besides being phenomenally influential and fundamentally rooted in the notion of power, is that they all see Jesus' crucifixion as an illustration of something we have plenty of other ways of knowing. Their accounts of human behaviour and society are so all-encompassing that they're like a science – they have no significant room for exceptions; still less a unique, definitive moment that reveals the truth about humanity and God and sets the entire agenda for their future interaction. It's not that most people know in detail what these figures propounded, it's that their collective legacy has passed into the public imagination, in an abiding cynicism about ideals, suspicion about truth, and assumption about hidden or subconscious agendas, reduced in some cases to money, sex and power. And, in a different way from what we've seen hitherto, this leaves the cross hanging by a thread.

Why? Because if we take Jesus' cross to be the unique, defining moment in history, then sure, we see its physical agony, we appreciate its emotional torment, we understand its monstrous injustice, we comprehend its overwhelming horror – but it reveals everything, and even more importantly changes everything: and so we can come to terms with it as the shadow that falls over time, the better to see the light. But if the crucifixion is at best an illustration of a general truth, and at worst an egregious sign of an ethic gone seriously wrong, a punishment that shouldn't have been given or a sacrifice that should have been profoundly resisted – then it becomes truly unbearable, pointless, pathetic, pitiable, sad. Why on earth would we gather to worship a person who died in a gruesome but futile gesture against all that's wrong with the world? We might keep vigil, and stand in solidarity – but in the end it would be no more than a celebration of glorious, perhaps misguided, failure. And it would turn out Nietzsche was right.

Again there are two ways Christians can respond to this. The first is defensive. It's to say seeking power is as empty as making yourself the biggest bully in the playground: it gives you the ability to impact others more than they can damage you, but it gives you nothing in the face of the challenges we've been looking at – trust, life and purpose. It can't buy you love, you can't take it with you, and it doesn't help you make sense of anything. In other words; if you judge yourself by your power, you're defining yourself by the wrong thing – by a diamond that quickly turns to dust.

All of which is true, but offers little consolation. What's more true, and is perhaps the only way to respond to these narratives of power, is to see that Jesus is exercising power, but a different kind of power. In his book *Speaking of God* (London: SPCK 1992, pp. 80–82), Trevor Dennis tells of a scene of desolation. He describes a stale, stinking canal, broken lamp-posts, flats boarded up. No grass, and no trees. Graffiti everywhere. For 30 years the site had been empty since an explosion killed Mabel and Arthur, asleep in their bed in the front room downstairs. No one had ever found their bodies. Nothing grew there, until one autumn a seed took root. Nobody noticed the plant for several weeks, but in the end you can't miss a sunflower. There it stood, five or six feet tall, with its heavy, golden head. Most of the local people had never seen a sunflower. Some were changed by its beauty. They no longer had that tired, dejected stoop, so characteristic of the inhabitants of those streets. Most people, however, were merely bewildered. It was so out of place.

The people left the sunflower alone. They thought they'd get used to it. But they couldn't. It showed up the drabness, the desolation all around for what it was: empty, ugly, dead. So people grew bitter about it. It became intolerable. One evening they went in a great crowd and they trampled on that sunflower, and danced on it, and beat the fibres of its leaves and stem, and crushed its petals. Then they went away in silence. And yet the people destroyed that plant in high summer, when its flower was full of ripe seed. In their dance of death they scattered that seed over the entire site, and buried some of it in the ground. So it was that next spring what had been a scene of desolation was covered with sunflowers. There were flowers on Mabel and Arthur's grave at last.

There's a power at work in this story, but not the power that Nietzsche assumes or Freud detects or Foucault unveils or Marx discloses. It's not about force, or coercion or my-daddy's-bigger-than-your-daddy. It's partly about using the energy of evil against itself.

But beyond that is the ability to disclose the end of the story in the middle of the story. The great debate about the cross in historical theology is about whether it objectively changes *God's* heart, by offering a sufficient sacrifice to deliver us from God's wrath, or whether it subjectively changes *our* hearts, by showing us once for all how much God loves us. But it's the wrong debate. It assumes what we can't recognize, that the all-powerful God should preordain the horrifying death of Christ – in other words that God should contradict the character we worship and adore in order to achieve something arbitrary and abstract.

Instead, this is what I believe the cross is. God always intended Jesus to come among us. Not to fix a problem, but to embody God's love. Incarnation came with a risk – a risk that Jesus would be treated like the sunflower in the story. When that risk was realized, God did not slink away, lash out, or call time. Instead, God underwent the full and horrifying consequences of that risk. But God also did one more thing. God disclosed the way the story ends. The way the story ends was decided before the story began. And that's how God exposes the emptiness of power. For power is the ability to achieve desired outcomes. But the final outcome, more than we desire or deserve, has already been decided.

So yes, the cross is a scene of desolation, desperation and despair. It shows the pointlessness, finality and untrustworthiness of existence. But it also gives us a glimpse of how the story will end, of how God will finally turn despondency into sunflowers and destruction into glory. Good Friday is the day we look back, and see how profoundly God has always loved us, and how allergic we've always been to that love and purpose. Easter is the day we look forward, to when the story finally comes to an end, when evil disappears into a black hole, when all doomed quests for power collapse into a big crunch, and we become seeds in a glowing sunflower.

And linking Good Friday, Easter and end of the story – the worst day, the best day and the last day – there's a narrow, fragile but precious thread. The thread is called Jesus. It's the thread our faith hangs on. It's our salvation.

6

Love

We've seen that the conventional ways of talking about the cross, as a sacrifice that satisfies justice or a ransom that appeases Satan, or even as a gesture that moves our souls, all run into trouble in the face of history, trust, life, purpose and power. And yet the cross hangs on, Jesus hangs on, by a thread, and on that thread hangs our salvation. In this last chapter I want to challenge the idea that the cross was a ghastly necessity that achieved a wonderful result. I want to explore how it was a wondrous gift that was all of a piece with the wondrous love it disclosed.

The 2012 Jesse Andrews' novel, also a 2015 Alfonso Gomez-Rejon film, *Me and Earl and the Dying Girl,* introduces us to gawky drifter Greg, in his final year at high school, in Pittsburgh. He can't find a way to form a real relationship with anybody, except Earl, with whom he makes short films, all of which parody other, better known films. Greg's parents learn that his childhood friend, Rachel, has contracted leukaemia, and they cajole him into visiting her. In an excruciating scene, two awkward teenagers, one facing death, the other without the skills of relating, eventually manage to establish a tentative conversation. Eager to support Greg, Earl persuades him to show Rachel the collection of short films, which she enjoys. Greg starts to spend more time with Rachel. As she begins chemotherapy, Greg and Earl start making a film for her. It takes up most of their time and Greg misses a lot of school.

In the film's decisive scene, Rachel tells Greg she's decided to stop the chemotherapy because it was doing more harm than good. They have a terrible argument, and Greg stops visiting her. Earl also breaks his friendship with Greg, criticizing his inability to care for anyone but himself. Months pass, and Greg is all dressed up to attend the high school prom with the girl of his dreams. But instead of going to the ball, he heads instead to the hospice where Rachel is languishing. Greg lies beside her on her deathbed, and shows her the film he and Earl made for her, which moves her deeply. Soon she lapses into a coma; shortly afterwards she dies. After the funeral Greg finds in Rachel's bedroom a host of kind and thoughtful gestures that Rachel left for him.

The film is a study in what it means to be *with* one another. At the start, Greg is incapable of being with anybody, including himself. He's able to work with Earl, but only so as to make fun of others. Greg is forced to be with Rachel, but while their relationship is based on pity it founders. Only when it's grounded in humour and common observation does it begin to flower. Not content with being *with* her, Greg resolves to do something *for* her – make a movie. The irony is that, short as her days are, the time working for her diminishes his time being with her. The crucial moment comes when Rachel decides to discontinue chemotherapy. Greg is furious because she's burst the bubble of his optimism. He really thought he could coach her back to health. She says that's not how it's going to be. Being with her means accompanying her to death. Greg refuses to believe it. He can't bear to stay with the story if it doesn't have a happy ending. He cuts off the *with* when it's most needed. Their friendship, like her life, is hanging by a thread.

But at the climax, when Greg has the choice between the romantic *with* of his beautiful date, and the deeper *with* of going to the hospice, he comes to his senses. As he lies beside Rachel on her deathbed he shares the film, and her tears are a recognition that, in his clumsiness, he did do something beautiful for her, which was a kind of love, even if not the kind she most wanted and needed. But now that finally he's discovered the meaning of *with*, she dies. Afterwards Greg discovers that, since he wouldn't give Rachel the *with*, she'd resorted to *for* gestures of her own. They were also gestures of love; but finding them, he realizes what, in his determination to be her saviour, he lost in failing to be her companion.

We try to make the cross the ultimate *for* – the consummate gesture that the God who worked for us in creation and exodus finally makes to secure the salvation of Israel and extend it to the whole world. But this drives a wedge between the God we see revealed in Christ in the Gospels, the God who identifies with us, walks with us, inhabits our green pastures, still waters, and places of danger, and asks us to walk with him to Jerusalem, to Calvary, to the cross – and the God who fixes our problem with sin and death but emerges bloodied and bowed from the fight.

In *Me and Earl and the Dying Girl* all the gestures of *for* are failures. Greg's attempt to have pity is rejected; the making of the film actually distances the two teenagers from one another; the chemotherapy fails. What matters is the *with* – the companionship amid adversity, the challenge Earl makes to Greg about whether he's willing to be part of an unhappy story, and finally the reconciliation on the hospice bed. If we insist on a God who's *for* us, we distance ourselves, instrumentalize God, problematize the whole relationship, invoke arcane notions of justice, and end up turning God the Father into a bloodthirsty monster. Isn't it time we realized the story is from beginning to end about *with*? God began the story out of a longing to be our companion. The billions of years of Big Bang and cosmological wonders weren't enough. God wanted to be with one that could respond, befriend, comprehend. For sure, that entailed being on the receiving end of betrayal, denial, weakness, flight. But all the more God felt compelled to be with us in person, to be among and alongside and together and amidst. And the cross shows us how deeply we resist God being with us, yet how willing God is at any cost to be with us regardless.

And this paradox is perfectly expressed in the scene of the two thieves talking to Jesus on the cross. The first thief can only perceive Jesus as a failed version of working *for*: 'Are you not the Messiah? Save yourself and us!' But the second thief realizes that there's something deeper going on than a cosmic plumber fixing a burst heavenly pipe. He says, 'Jesus, remember me when you come into your kingdom.' Note that – he doesn't say, 'Save me.' He says 'Remember me.' In other words, 'May I be with you even when you're gone from here.' And what does Jesus say? 'Today you will be with me in Paradise.' Being *with* is what it was all about. God being with us is what creation, exodus, covenant and cross are all about. Being *with* is what eternity is all about. And you don't have to wait for ever for it: you can have it today. The suffering of the cross can't take it away from you. The depth of your failure and folly and fecklessness can't deprive you of it. The barrier of death is not stronger that its power. Being *with* is paradise. And you can have it today.

For the centuries of Christendom the cross was seen as an answer. Life held only two fundamental challenges – sin and death – and the cross dealt with them as surely as restoring sight and comfort by taking a speck of dust out of an eye. But the end of Christendom and the accumulated challenges of history, trust, life, purpose and power have turned the cross from an answer into a question. The cross is not a half-baked, ham-fisted or half-immoral attempt to rescue, ransom or redeem us from sin, death or evil. It's a harrowing exposure of the depravity of our sin, a definitive demonstration of God's perpetual purpose, a unique revelation of God's wondrous love, an ultimate disclosure of our destiny with God, and an astonishing invitation to be with Christ in paradise.

Standing before the cross we face the same decision Greg faced the day Rachel gave up her chemotherapy. Are we willing to be part of this story, even if it isn't a rescue story, even if in many ways it's a sad story? Are we willing to be with the God who's given everything to be with us? Maybe, like Greg, we wander off, angry, self-righteous, grieving, bewildered. Our faith, our hope, our love, are hanging by a thread. But maybe like Greg, when it matters most, we come back, and resolve to be with Jesus. Because, in the end, there's no other story we have any desire to live by.

7

Story

The 2005 John Boyne novel, also a 2008 Mark Herman film, *The Boy in the Striped Pyjamas*, is set in Germany during the Second World War. Bruno is an eight-year-old boy whose father is a soldier in the Nazi war machine. Early in the film, Bruno and his family move to another part of Germany, where Bruno's father has become the commandant of a strange kind of camp. Bruno is often alone, and eager to find things to do. Eventually he wanders out of the back yard and meanders beyond the wood, and finds a high fence. Within the fence there are people, and those people seem to be wearing striped pyjamas.

Bruno walks up to the fence and sees a boy about his own age. He introduces himself and finds that the other boy is called Shmuel. He's fascinated by Shmuel and they have an intriguing conversation and he arranges to come back and talk some more, which he does repeatedly. The two boys play draughts through the fence and talk about many things, often having to break off their conversation for fear of being discovered. Bruno can't fully understand why Shmuel is incarcerated, why he has to wear pyjamas, why he's so thin and so hungry, and what role his own father has in all of this. Gradually the tension in Bruno's own home intensifies as his mother and sister come to realize what's really going on in the camp. One day Bruno gets a surprise: he's playing in his home and sees Shmuel working as a cleaner in the dining room. Bruno gives Shmuel some food. But a soldier interrupts them and demands to know why Shmuel is eating and where he got the food from. Bruno panics and says, 'I don't know – I've never seen him before.'

Bruno quickly regrets his words and soon returns to the fence, hoping to see Shmuel and be reconciled. The large black eye on Shmuel's face tells the price Shmuel paid for Bruno's betrayal. But Shmuel accepts Bruno's apology. Bruno's father finally accepts that this is no place to bring up children and arranges for his wife and family to move elsewhere. For Bruno this means the terrible prospect of leaving Shmuel. So he goes to visit Shmuel at the fence. Shmuel has got some pyjamas for Bruno to wear so he can blend into the camp and not be taken away with his family. Bruno scrambles under the fence and into the camp and dons a striped hat so no one can tell his head is unshaven. The two boys set about searching for Shmuel's father, who's missing.

Suddenly the atmosphere changes. Soldiers appear, corralling large groups of people in striped pyjamas towards the large barn at one end of the camp. There's no escape, and Bruno and Shmuel are swept up into the crowd. All the people are herded like cattle down the steps and into the barn. At this point Bruno's mother discovers he's missing and sounds the alarm. A host of soldiers start looking for Bruno. But it's too late. He's in the barn beside Shmuel, and all the people in the barn are being told to take off their clothes, ready for a shower. It's clear they realize this is going to be no ordinary shower, but the full horror of what lies ahead dawns on the prisoners, on Bruno's family, and on the reader and viewer, all at the same time. Somehow both knowing and not knowing the terrible truth, Bruno and Shmuel clasp hands and squeeze tight, and it's clear that nothing in the world could persuade them to let go. As the darkness descends and the gas begins to be pumped in and the horror engulfs the barn, Bruno says, 'You're my best friend, Shmuel. My best friend for life.'

It's a children's story. But it's not a children's story. It's a story about mass murder, deception, a nation's ability to hide the truth from itself and others, merciless cruelty, systematic genocide, apocalyptic slaughter and indescribable suffering. But at the heart of the story lie two boys who become friends because they don't know any better, vividly displaying the irony that they know better than anyone. They in fact are the only ones who do know better. The centre of the film is the contrast between on the one hand the two communities on opposite sides of the fence, divided by oppression and lies and vicious evil and appalling cruelty and organized annihilation, and on the other hand the two boys, clasping each other's hand as they face their deaths, knowing nothing more truly than the indivisibility of their hearts and the inseparability of their destinies, defined by trust and friendship and forgiveness and love.

I want to suggest to you that this story, this narrative of Bruno and Shmuel side by side, is really a picture of God and us. It's the story of incarnation and cross. Jesus enters the camp of danger with every likelihood that his entry will sooner or later entail his gruesome execution. Jesus takes on the garment of exclusion and prepares to face the consequences of humanity's rejection of God. Jesus becomes a Jew and discovers for himself the reviling and persecution Jews have known throughout the ages. Jesus becomes a little child and places himself at the mercy of adults who can't be trusted to have any idea what they're doing. Fundamentally, when we're surrounded by chaos, in the midst of hell, at the mercy of cruel powers, terrified, naked, humiliated and helpless, Jesus is right beside us, saying, 'You're my best friend. My best friend for life. I wouldn't be anywhere else in the world but right here beside you.'

That's what those mysterious words of John's Gospel mean. 'The Word became flesh and lived among us.' God didn't just create us, didn't just love us from afar, didn't just work in history to rescue us and strengthen us and heal us. God's real glory, God's true nature, appears in the real, substantial, material, physical reality of Jesus among us, Jesus just like us, Jesus beside us. And beside us not just in joy and celebration, but beside us in horror, in agony, in isolation, in abandonment. Jesus is Bruno, donning the pyjamas, reshaping his whole life to be beside us, coming inside the camp of obliteration when he could just as easily have remained outside; but Jesus is just as much Shmuel, carrying that black eye, forgiving us when he's suffered for our sin, the Jew who includes even ignorant Gentiles in the solidarity of salvation.

Whose hand is holding yours in the chaos and mayhem and terror of your world? Who has gone out of their way to stand next to you? Who has been brave enough to make you their friend, has forgiven you when you turned your back on them, has come alongside and worn your clothes and faced the reality of your existence and known the fear that you thought was yours alone? We can have all the knowledge and learning we like, but sometimes it takes a little boy, maybe a little boy wearing striped pyjamas, to show us the answer to those questions. The most important choice we make is who you make your friends. Not just people who are useful to you; not just those who are interesting, or similar, or funny, or beautiful: but those in whose hands lies the secret of your soul.

The Christian faith is this: despite our meanness, despite our faithlessness, despite the danger and disgrace of doing so, God chose to become our friend. The one standing beside us in the gas chamber, saying we're his friend for ever and clasping our hand and never letting us go, is Jesus. And the day we discover the wonder, the glory, the mystery and the power of that is the day we decide to don the striped pyjamas – and become God's friends; now, and for ever.